FAITH
PROOF

Power to Resist Opposing Forces

Shontel D. Wood

WESTBOW
PRESS®
A DIVISION OF THOMAS NELSON
& ZONDERVAN

WestBow Press books may be ordered through booksellers or by contacting:

WestBow Press
A Division of Thomas Nelson & Zondervan
1663 Liberty Drive
Bloomington, IN 47403
www.westbowpress.com
844-714-3454

Because of the dynamic nature of the Internet, any web addresses or links contained in this book may have changed since publication and may no longer be valid. The views expressed in this work are solely those of the author and do not necessarily reflect the views of the publisher, and the publisher hereby disclaims any responsibility for them.

Any people depicted in stock imagery provided by Getty Images are models, and such images are being used for illustrative purposes only. Certain stock imagery © Getty Images.

Scripture quotations marked KJV are taken from the King James Version.

Scripture quotations marked NIV are taken from The Holy Bible, New International Version®, NIV® Copyright © 1973, 1978, 1984, 2011 by Biblica, Inc.® Used by permission. All rights reserved worldwide.

Scripture quotations marked ESV taken from The Holy Bible, English Standard Version® (ESV®), Copyright © 2001 by Crossway, a publishing ministry of Good News Publishers. All rights reserved.

ISBN: 978-1-9736-7407-8 (sc)
ISBN: 978-1-9736-7408-5 (e)

Library of Congress Control Number: 2019913461

Print information available on the last page.

WestBow Press rev. date: 08/28/2020

Contents

Dedication

I dedicate this book to my son, Darrel S. Wood. You have seen where your faith in God can take you. Remember, there is no limit to how far you can succeed in life for with God all things are possible. Keep pressing forward! I love you, Ma

Introduction

I want to encourage those that will read this book to stretch
your faith. Believe God for the impossible and do not allow
your past to keep you from having the successful future that
God intended for you. You have an opportunity of a lifetime.
An opportunity to be someone great, make something great or
do something great. It is sometimes difficult to rise above the
reality of what we see and push toward what we cannot see.
However, having faith will cause your dreams and visions to
come alive. Nothing is too hard for God, and as you trust Him,
you can achieve whatever you put your hands to do. Blessings!

Believing Is Seeing

"Now faith is the substance of things hoped for, the evidence of things not seen." Hebrews 11:1 (KJV)

When I think about faith, I believe the impossible becoming possible. As it pertains to spirituality, faith, as defined in the Merriam Webster Dictionary, is a "belief and trust in and loyalty to God." Hebrews 11: 1 declares that faith is right now. It is a presently existing state of being; the belief that God exists although we cannot see or touch Him. If you are going to believe God for anything, you must have faith to receive what you believe for.

Proof used as an adjective means able to resist or repel. To resist or repel means to exert force in opposition or fight against. In life, we face many opposing forces. Whether it be in our families, on our jobs, in school, ministry, or whatever it may be, we all have been opposed at one time or another. I know what it feels like to battle certain situations. It is like you are in a fight that feels like it will never end. Fighting for my success throughout my life became the norm for me, and it did not seem that I could get any good breaks. However, I knew I could not give up because giving up to me meant I would lose this fight. Proverbs 13: 12 (NKJV) says, "Hope deferred makes the heart sick, But when the desire comes, it is a tree of life." I finally got to a place where I was determined and had enough stamina to get up and keep moving forward.

Knowing God was with me; keeping me and strengthening me every day is what kept me going. However, I did not always feel that God was with me, and it was at those times where I felt that life had become intensified. It was so intense that at times, I felt suicidal. In my mind, I was feeling defeated. I was losing the will to go on further. I was in bad relationships, dealing with family struggles and nowhere near where I wanted to be. Life had taken its toll on me, and I decided it was best that I not be here any longer, and suicide was my only answer. With all of my struggles, I was pregnant with my son, and at that time, even he was not enough for me to live. I was depressed, and it was a very dark place, but in the back of my mind, this thought kept coming to me that "you cannot do this." It was not until later on that I realized that that was the voice of God speaking to me and intervening to save my life. I never knew that my life was worth saving up until that point. With strength and the power of God, I was able to overcome suicidal thoughts.

There are many opposing forces in life, and it's not just people that come to fight against you, but it is also the negative thoughts you rehearse over in your mind, which is a battle all in itself. You have to make a decision and choose to feed on the positive things. It can be somewhat challenging to focus on the positive at but what you put into daily practice becomes habits. Believing is a very crucial factor in opposing your adversary. You have to know and believe that you are able, even when it does not look favorable. Prayer, mixed with faith is what gets you through battles. You must have a prayer life if you intend to live a blessed and prosperous life. Pray believing that what you are praying for is already done. If you do not believe in what you are praying for them nine times out of ten, you will not see the manifestation of your prayer.

Mark 11:24 (NKJV) says "Therefore I say to you, whatever things you ask when you pray, believe that you receive them, and you will have them.", so if we're going to pray we must believe. Prayer is powerful to the believer. It sets your day, and it cancels the plans of the enemy over your life. Remember what you practiced becomes habits, and prayer is a perfect habit to have.

"Faithing it" is a term I use to remind myself that in all I do is by faith. Faith is in me, and it is a part of my DNA. I breathe faith, I walk by faith, and I speak by faith, knowing that any dreams I have according to God's will and purpose will come to pass. My substantial proof is that my faith is working for me in areas I cannot see.

Whenever you have a dream or a vision of something that you desire to do that's deep inside of you, there will be obstacles and hindrances to stop you from proceeding, but it is not an indication that you shouldn't, it is more of a sign that you should. With any big assignment that God is gracing you to do, it's going to come with great resistance, and with great resistance, there must be faith to move beyond what is opposing you.

3 John 1:2 (NKJV) declares that "Beloved, I pray that you may prosper in all things and be in health, just as your soul prospers" so God desires that we prosper and not just in material things but prospering in our faith as well.

It requires faith to get up every day and to move forward even when you do not feel like it or when you cannot see a way out of a situation you may be in. Having faith gives us the ability and the power to make things happen in the world that we live in. Without faith, some of the greatest inventions would have never been invented. Karl Benz was the first who invented the modern-day automobile. He had an idea to make something that he never made before, and he did. He created something that many of us are benefiting from today. He had a dream to make something wonderful, and he did. Look how big his dream became. There are countless cars today because of this one invention. See, you may think your dream is little or that it may not amount to anything, but I want you to stretch you vision beyond where you are and see your dream so big that even you cannot contain it alone.

Being rejected or denied is not a good feeling, and most of us have experienced this at some time in life. You may have had a good idea or a dream and attempted to get it started but was told "no" or "it'll never work." That can be very discouraging but just because you received a no, does it mean never? Sometimes some perfecting is needed and necessary wisdom to be gained. Sometimes your dreams need to be fine-tuned before you put out there. Therefore, when things do not work out as planned do not do what is most comfortable and quit but reassess, take a step back and revisit it. In the step back time, ask God to give you another view or a different perspective of what you are doing or trying to do and wait for Him to show you.

You cannot rush faith; it comes as we go along our daily living. As you trust in yourself and God, you will begin to see things unfold more positively. Have you ever been blindfolded and had to find your way by following someone's in front or behind you? Well, walking by faith is kind of like that. You cannot see how you will get to your destination, but you trust God that He will lead and guide you as you go.

Prayer: Dear God help me to have faith in you and to believe that all things are possible. Help me to trust you as you guide me through this life and help me to believe for what is bigger than in my ability to do and give me the power to produce what was nothing into something in Jesus name Amen.

Jumping

"Fear not, for I am with you; be not dismayed, for I am your God; I will strengthen you, I will help you, I will uphold you with my righteous right hand." Isaiah 41:10 (NKJV)

Jumping as it pertains to your faith is not as easy as it seems. A person who does not know how to swim will not just jump into a pool. No, they are usually far away from the pool, but a swimmer will go to the deep end of the pool and jump in without any care in the world. Fear of what's going to happen will keep you from jumping. I remember when I learned how to swim. My big brothers taught me, and although it was the unconventional way of teaching me by just throwing me in the deep end of the pool, they were there to make sure I did not drown. I trusted them even though I was scared, but I learned how to swim that day. God is the same with us. He tests our faith so that it will be proven, but also in that, He wants us to know that He is there with us always. God tests our faith so that it may be perfected and mature for what is to come.

Your faith is activated when you jump. Jump into what? Jump into God's purpose for your life. If you ever desire to become someone great in life or to do something that will have a significant impact or influence in the world, then it will require you to jump. Over analyzing can hinder your progression. Some people tend to overthink plans, visions, or dreams, which can eventually die because they have rehearsed repeatedly in their minds what could go wrong before they have even started. They worry about how it will turn out while trying to make it perfect. You cannot worry and have faith at the same time. One will supersede the other. It is either faith will conquer worry or worry will overcome faith. Do not allow overthinking to rob you out of something good. You cannot predict the outcome of a thing, but you can change how you think about it by thinking positively. Having positive people around you that will encourage and support you, will help keep you on track and balanced in your thinking.

One thing about the physical aspects of jumping is you have to use force to jump. Muscles are involved in jumping. You are using your legs, arms and feet to jump and so it is the same with faith; you have to have enough strength and trust to do whatever it is you put your mind to, and you have to do it without wavering. You cannot stop a jump in mid-air. You cannot have faith to jump and in the middle of the leap change your mind. James 1:8 (KJV) says, "A double-minded man *is* unstable in all his ways." You cannot be wishy-washy in your faith. You cannot be today in faith and then tomorrow confused. Your mind has to be convinced that no matter what comes or what happens, you will stand firm in the faith.

I remember when I went to college after being out of school for about 18 years. One of the biggest reasons for me continuing my education was to pave the way for my son to follow. I wanted to be that example that if I can then so can he. So, I started college, and the courses were very intense and accelerated. Before I made up my mind to go to college after so many years had passed, I also made up so many reasons why I could not or why I should not. I was a single parent. I was working full-time, and to me, that was a lot, and I didn't see how that was possible.

Now here I was, considering adding accelerated college courses to my life. I had put it off for so long by telling myself I'll do it later until later became days, months, and years. Then, one day, I just jumped. I jumped right into furthering my education. I stopped thinking about it over and over, and I did it.

See, sometimes the delay is because of our procrastination. We say that we are waiting for something good to happen when the good we are waiting on is in us to make it happen. We put off visions and dreams because of life situations. We say, "When I get more money, then I'll do this" or "After the kids are older, then I'll open my own business." but my question to you is why wait? Usually, when we keep delaying something, we don't start it at all, or it becomes just a memory of something that could have been. Do not let your dreams die but, work on them, and put it in action.

Back to the college story, when I called the school to ask about the courses, and as the advisor was explaining and as I listened, I was already thinking defeat in my mind, I kept saying, "this is going to be hard." My biggest fear was starting and not finishing. However, I told the advisor to sign me up. I started, and it was not easy. It was a challenging time of my life, but I refused to quit in the middle but to go all the way and complete it. I thank the Lord for giving me the strength to get through it and grateful for my family for being a support system during this time but one thing that was a reminder and motivator was the "why." Why was I doing this, and every time I wanted to quit, I would remember that this is not just about me but also my family.

It was those moments I felt a push to continue to the end. I encourage you to focus on one or two positive motivators whenever you set a goal or when you have made a decision to pursue your dreams. Think about those when you reach the point of weariness and when you feel like giving up. The momentum you used to get [jump] off the ground has to be what you focus on to get you where you are going. You don't jump haphazardly. You jump with a purpose. I am grateful to say; I finished college with honors a year before my son graduated high school. My son soon followed and went to college. He completed it and graduated with his bachelor's degree.

Jumping is just not about you, but it is about those that are connected to you and those whose path you will cross. I could not see all the details of this jump entirely, but I knew in my heart I had to do it and it was so worth it. Not only did the jump open the way for my son but it also promoted me in my profession, and it gave me something that no one could ever take away from me; it gave me a testimony that I could finally say, "I did it!"

God will make provision for you when you trust Him. I remember years ago, God was dealing with me regarding relocating to another state. I had lived where I was born and raised all my life, and I had a desire to relocate. I prayed and prayed seeking direction from the Lord as to how and when. Moving to another state was something I never did before, and it was unfamiliar to me. God began confirming this move through little signs, but I was still very hesitant because I would be leaving all that I knew for something new. This was a faith move because I was going to be starting life in a new place. As much as I question was this the right move? I was ready to jump. I remember giving my job at the time a two weeks' notice, and it was at that moment things became real.

This relocation was really about to happen. I could not back out of it now and nor did I want to because now I was more interested in seeing the outcome of this move. My fear turned into excitement as I trusted and believed God that he would do something beautiful in this move. To add to this, a previous job I worked at almost five years before this move sent a certified letter stating that they owed me money from all those years ago. This happened after I decided to go forward and relocate by faith. God had made provision for the move before I had all the pieces together. He provided for us, and it was more than enough to sustain us. Sometimes God is waiting on us to do something never done before to prove to that He is with us along the way. You cannot be immobile and expect to see the world. The only way you will see places you have never seen before is if you go. There are things you may want to do that you have put off. I encourage you to put it off no longer and start again.

Prayer: Dear God, please remove all fear that would mobilize me for you have not given a spirit of fear but of power and a sound mind. Give me the strength and confidence to believe in myself and the courage to overcome any obstacle in Jesus name Amen.

The Unknown

"For I know the thoughts that I think toward you, says the Lord, thoughts of peace and not of evil, to give you a future and a hope." Jeremiah 29:11 (NKJV)

One of the biggest hindrances I believe that keeps people from not pursuing their dreams is fear of the unknown. It is easy if you knew beforehand how things would work out. We tend to need to know all the details and turns before we make a conscious decision to go. In Genesis 12:1 (NKJV), God told Abraham, "Get out of your country, From your family And from your father's house, To a land that I will show you." Imagine being told to pack up your house, all of your belongings and load them in the truck because you're moving. Our first instinct is to respond, "Where am I moving to?" We want to know or should I say we have to know it all before we ever move.

Knowing is like having that special blanket you always get to help you get comfortable. Knowing gives us something to lean on as we go, and it soothes our emotions. Knowing either excites you or causes you to fold and bunker down in fear but knowing isn't always good. Some things need to be unknown for our sanity. Right now, can you think of something that if you knew all the details beforehand would you have continued with it or say never mind?

Although the bible does not mention it, but I imagined when Abraham was told to leave his country that he wrestled in his mind with all kinds of thoughts and questions regarding his future. In Genesis 12:2-3 (NKJV), God told Abraham that He was going to make him a great nation and that he would be abundantly blessed. With hearing all the good things that were going to come we still wrestle with the unknown of the details. We don't know what we will face on the way however, there's something key that God told Abraham in Genesis 12:3 (NKJV) He said "I will bless those who bless you, and I will curse him who curses you; And in you all the families of the earth shall be blessed." This was a declaration and a promise of protection and generational blessings for Abraham and his family. Abraham's future was secured. On hearing this, Abraham faithfully and in full obedience to God made a move. Everything may not make sense at the time you proceed forward in your dreams and aspirations, but the first step if the faith-step. You must take the first step!

As crazy as your dream may be unless you take the first step towards it, it will just remain an excellent idea. However, when you consider that step forward; you will have the desire to continue to see more.

In each step, you learn something that will bring the dream into fulfillment and manifestation. When I went back to school, I did not see all the benefits when I took the first step, but the last step was so rewarding. Just like Abraham, not only was I blessed, but also my family was blessed and reaped the benefits of my faith.

Step out into the unknown. It is easy to go where you are familiar with because you are used to a particular place. It poses no challenge to you because you have become so familiar with it. The moment things become uncertain, or it looks strange, that is when we become immobilized.

Uncharted territory can be very intimidating, but that is when you have to faith proof your circumstances. What do I mean by faith proof? I mean to pull out the protection that covers and empowers you in your thinking and put it on. Put on a positive mindset and rehearse positivity until you feel confident in yourself. Philippians 4:8 (ESV) says "Finally, brothers, whatever is true, whatever is honorable, whatever is just, whatever is pure, whatever is lovely, whatever is commendable, if there is any excellence, if there is anything worthy of praise, think about these things." Our thoughts shape our destiny. To receive greater, you have to think higher. What we continuously think about will eventually manifest. So, if you are always thinking negatively about your situations or even people, then that's all you will see.

If you practice thinking on good things and meditating on those things that are positive, you will begin to see the fruit of it. Negative thoughts will come and when they do address it, pull it down, and then replace it with what God says about you in His word. If you can never see yourself doing anything significant you more than likely will never do anything that will make you great; but if you feed your mind with what is commendable, you will be motivated to be great, and you will start doing great things.

Lastly, we have to know that God's plan for our lives is good. His thoughts are never evil when He thinks about us because evil is not in Him. The moment we realize and believe that God wants the best life for us more than we could ever wish for ourselves is when we will begin to see His great plan unfold right before our eyes.

Prayer: Dear God lead me on the path you have for me and let me not go astray. Be my compass when I am at a crossroad and led me on higher ground. Help me to trust that your plans are good for me in Jesus name Amen.

Trust Factor

"For we walk by faith, not by sight." 2 Corinthians 5:7 (NKJV)

It is so hard to trust a path or a plan you never been on before. Proverbs 3:5-6 (NKJV) says "Trust in the Lord with all your heart, And lean not on your own understanding; In all your ways acknowledge Him, And He shall direct your paths." We have to first submit to God for His guidance. Submitting is not a slave mentality because He gives all have free will to choose, but submission is accepting His will for our lives is better than what we can do. Our understanding can be limited and sometimes misleading. Too often, people are led by their emotions when God wants us to be led by His Spirit. God wants us to rely on His power and wisdom for complicated affairs we face. He wants us to trust His sovereignty for our lives.

Walking by faith is challenging, but it is not impossible. We see things happening all around us that may be discouraging and appearing to be the total opposite of the dreams we envisioned. However, if we are going to do what we have never done before, we are going to have to trust God for what we cannot see. We must walk by faith and not by sight if we intend to reach our dreams in life. Faith opens the door to unlimited possibilities.

Trusting is not always easy to do, especially when it involves something new or unfamiliar. Broken trust can hinder and damage relationships, whether it is business or personal. It takes time for one to regain confidence again, but it is not impossible.

When Moses died, Joshua was the next in charge to lead the children of Israel across the Jordan River. Joshua had to finish what Moses started, and he had to fill some big shoes and was terrified and afraid. In Joshua 1:9 (NIV) God told Joshua, "Have I not commanded you? Be strong and courageous. Do not be afraid; do not be discouraged, for the LORD your God will be with you wherever you go." If I can imagine what Joshua went through when he was given instructions to lead the children of Israel, I imagined he was a nervous wreck. Maybe he was unsure of how things would turn out or if he would fail the people he was now leading. Twice God told Joshua to be strong and courageous, and I believe told him that because Joshua was having a hard time trusting God with the assignment that was now in his hands. However, God reassured Joshua that he could trust him by telling him not to be terrified because he was going to be with him wherever he went. From that point, there was trust between Joshua and God. Here, God is letting us know that as long as He is with us, we have no reason to be afraid of anything. When you put your trust in God, you will never be disappointed.

When situations look discouraging, we have to trust God will never leave or forsake us. Being in an unfavorable position will either cause you to turnaround and retreat, get stuck where you are or proceed forward with boldness.

It takes faith to trust what is unknown, and sometimes you have to be willing to take a risk to trust. Nobody wants to take a chance and not succeed, but sometimes it may take more than one try to be successful. The key is not giving up when things do not go as planned.

Believers in God live by faith and trust in Him. Though we cannot see Him, we believe He exists. Not only that, but He is concerned about our lives and He wants us to trust Him with it. God knows all things. He knows the ending from the beginning. If we are going to prosper in anything, we will have to learn to trust in Him. I did not always trust God because I could not see everything He was doing, but once I realized that He was teaching me how to walk by faith and not by sight, I knew I could trust Him with everything. When you are confused and unsure of life's direction, try God. We can seek many things for guidance, but the word of God is like a GPS. It gets us to our destinations, and it gets us there safely. The word of God will reroute you if you should go the wrong way or get lost. It cautions us when to slow down and when to stop. It puts us on the right track when we apply it. Apply the word of God to your life daily.

Prayer: Dear God teach me to trust you with all my heart and teach me to not lean to my own understanding. Help me to rely on you and help me to rely on your word as the ultimate source and give me perfect peace in Jesus name Amen.

Distractions

"Keep your eyes straight ahead; ignore all sideshow distractions." Proverbs 4:25 (MSG)

Distractions usually come to hinder you and get you off course from the thing you are focusing on. You may find that you started very excited and focused on something, and then little things started coming up to pull you away from what you have purposed to do. Those little things become big things that cause delays from what you have set out to do. If you do not refocus and get back on track, you can find yourself never completing what you have started.

Being distracted can lead to you being discouraged, which can lead to you becoming disoriented about what your goal and dreams are. You may find yourself questioning if this is something that you are supposed to do. Being distracted can cause you to lose your sense of direction or have you confused, and "God is not the author of confusion." 1 Corinthians 14:33 (KJV) Distractions have one purpose, and that is to get you to discontinue what you have started to do.

Distractions are disruptions that cause delays. We live in a hectic world where things are always happening around us. It is effortless to get distracted. When it pertains to your purpose and destiny, distractions come to derail and stop you, but you have to be vigilant in pursuing your goal. You have to be very observant and alert so that you aware of things that pull you away from your purpose.

Distractions are like time stealers, they subtly creep in presenting itself as the main attraction, and before you realize it, you are attending to it. You have forgotten all about what you were doing first, and by the time it comes back to your mind, you have wasted time. It is ok to focus on one thing at a time. I know some can multitask and of course, you can multitask. However, depending on how big or important the project, task, or goal is to you, you would want to finish it with little to none distractions.

If you are working on more than one thing at a time, it would be best to prioritize them according to their importance and work on them in that order. Whatever happens, do not stop and do not quit. There should be minimum breaks until you reach that finish line. If you want the reward, you have to persevere to the end. It may not feel great or encouraging, but the outcome and the feeling of completion is joyful.

When a horse is in a race, they usually wear horse blinders to prevent them from seeing behind or beside them. Those horse blinders are distraction blockers to keep the horse focused on the finish line ahead. It also keeps them from concentrating on those things on the sidelines. That is what we have to do sometimes; we have to put on distraction blinders to help keep us focused on what is ahead. Everyone nowadays wants to be first to finish the race, but it is not always about finishing first as it is about finishing.

The truth is this; situations will arise that will interrupt the flow of what you are working on or trying to accomplish. Do not allow those things to frustrate you to the point you give up, but instead regroup, and let the peace of God rule in your heart. God's peace will settle you when trials come. The devil also uses these situations to get us off God's timetable to abort our destinies, but we have to be aware of his tricks and demolish his plans every time. Distractions are the biggest tool for the devil. He does not mind you getting started on something. His assignment is to keep you from finishing it. It is to hinder your progress, but you must persevere to the end.

Perseverance is being persistent in doing something, no matter the delay or difficulty. "The race is not always given to the swift and the battle is not always won by the strong but to the ones that endure to the end" Ecclesiastes 9:11 (KJV).

You may experience many disruptions but do not stall at the things that occur on the sidelines. Keep your attention on what is ahead of you. The real winners are those that have endured to the end.

Prayer: Dear God, keep my mind stayed on you and keep me in perfect peace so that when distractions come, I will not be overwhelmed. Help me to stay focused on you and what you have blessed me to do that it may bring you glory in Jesus name Amen.

Bridges

"I can do all things through Christ who strengthens me." Philippians 4:13 (NKJV)

A bridge is a structure that allows passage over a river, road, chasm or the like. I want to talk about bridges in regard to your faith. There are many types of bridges, but they all have the same purpose. However, going across a bridge requires much faith, determination, and focus.

I do not like bridges, and I despise crossing them. There are short bridges where you can see the other side, and there are long bridges where you cannot see the other side. Those long bridges are what I once feared. I would close my eyes when going over one. There are things in life, like bridges that can test our faith.

You have to choose whether to walk in fear or faith. Fear will suggest you should not do it, and faith will indicate that you can do it. Fear cripples you, whereas faith empowers you along the way reassuring you step by step. We usually fear what we do not understand. We fear what is uncommon to us, but if you ever want to do extraordinary things, you will need to have faith in God to help you cross the bridges in life. I know that is sometimes easy said than done but it is a reality that all of us are faced with at some point in our lives. I have dealt with fear many times and it still has a tendency to arise but I have to remind myself not to allow fear to win. Fear will show up at the most unexpected times in your life but you have to be ready and determine to not back away but to defeat it head on.

Bridges get you from one place to another. They get you from one destination to the other. They help you to get over difficult obstacles that would otherwise be hard to get over. We cross bridges that get us to our destinies. Without bridges, it would be challenging to reach the place that God intended for us. Do not despise bridges. Although, it may look scary, "you can do all things through Jesus Christ who gives you strength." Philippians 4:13 (NKJV) If God got you to the bridge, then He's more than able to get you across the bridge.

Notice that on some bridges you cannot make a u-turn. You have to go all the way once you're on the bridge. You cannot stop in the middle of the bridge, change your mind, and decide to go back, but you must go completely over the bridge, or you will never get to your destination. Now, view the bridge as your faith. See faith as that bridge you travel on that gets you over the difficulties that life brings. Just as the bridge helps us get to where we are going, so does our faith. Faith is the believers' passageway throughout life.

Choose faith over fear. God's plan for you is that you have a successful and prosperous life and to give you an expected end. The end does not mean that it is the end of all things, but it is the end of where you are now going from faith to faith where victory is your destination. When Moses and the children of Israel had to cross the Red Sea in Exodus 14:1-31 (NKJV), they could not even see across to where they were going. They reached what appeared to them an end, but it was a new beginning of something they had never experienced. It was brand new and unfamiliar, but there was no going back to where they came from because the enemy was chasing them to kill them. It was at that moment that faith kicked in because either the children of Israel trusted Moses with their lives enough to follow him or not and turn back and be killed. They trusted Moses because they were facing a place of no return. There was no escape route, no other way to turn to and be safe. God performed a miracle for the children of Israel by dividing the Red Sea for them to get away from their enemies. He responded to their faith and moved powerfully on their behalf.

Have you ever felt like you were backed into a corner and could not get out? Have you ever felt trapped in something with nowhere to go and you thought the worst? You felt like what is the use of fighting to survive? In those times when it seems you have reached a dead-end, trust God. Trust that He is with you to lead you on a path never traveled on. God responds to our faith. Faith is for the present and the future. You cannot have hope for something that has already happened. Having faith pushes you to press through the obstacles and challenges, knowing with assurance that the end will be victorious.

Prayer: Dear God, be the bridge I travel on that gets me to the promise that you have ordained for my life. Cancel all fear and replace it with boldness so that I will conquer and overcome all that oppose me in Jesus name Amen.

The Shield

"Above all, taking the shield of faith with which
you will be able to quench all the fiery darts of
the wicked one." Ephesians 6:16 (NKJV)

A shield is a defensive weapon usually worn on the arm of a soldier who was in battle. It was a Roman shield called the scutum. It was as large as a door, and it was big enough to cover a soldier's body. The shield was a soldier's most powerful weapon that was used to push back his enemies as well as cover him from arrows from above. It was sort of like a bulletproof vest that our police officers use today. It was protection for the soldier in battle. A bulletproof vest is a personal armor that helps absorb the impact and reduce or stop penetration to the body from firearm fired projectiles and shrapnel.

It sounds like a mighty weapon to use. Even with a powerful weapon like this, there was no guarantee of survival. The shield of faith is a spiritual weapon that you can possess that is not visible but very powerful. Ephesians 6:10-17 (KJV) says, "Finally, my brethren, be strong in the Lord and in the power of His might. Put on the whole armor of God, that you may be able to stand against the wiles of the devil. For we do not wrestle against flesh and blood, but against principalities, against powers, against the rulers of the darkness of this age, against spiritual hosts of wickedness in the heavenly places. Therefore take up the whole armor of God, that you may be able to withstand in the evil day, and having done all, to stand. Stand therefore, having girded your waist with truth, having put on the breastplate of righteousness, and having shod your feet with the preparation of the gospel of peace; above all, taking the shield of faith with which you will be able to quench all the fiery darts of the wicked one. And take the helmet of salvation, and the sword of the Spirit, which is the word of God."

Every piece of the armor described in the book of Ephesians Chapter 6 (KJV) has a particular role in protecting the saints from the wickedness of the devil. Verse 14 talks about having your loins girt about with truth in which the soldiers wore before going into battle. The belt they wore would hold their armor in place, and it also gave them a place to put their sword. It was the first piece of armor Paul mentioned in Ephesians 6 because it was the most important in its role. Without the belt, the armor was ineffective.

Today we wear belts to hold up our clothes to keep them from falling. Without out it our clothes would fall down, and then we would have to use our hand to keep them up. Which would be a distraction because you need your hands for other things. A belt goes around the waist, circling the entire body. This is how the truth of God's word circles all around us. It should encompass all around the believer. The belt of truth is the word of God that holds up the believer keeping him or her together by encouraging and exhorting one to stand firm in the truth of God's word. The word of God sustains the believer. The word of God is often referred to as the word of truth. It is important that we are walking in truth. God's word sanctifies us because it is true.

The breastplate was worn to protect from injuries to the upper body. The breastplate of righteousness here is doing what is right in God's eyes. It is the obedience of God's word against sin and unclean living. It is the love of God, showing us that He loves us. It is so crucial to be fully clothed, not just with material clothing but also with our spiritual garment as well. Being clothe spiritually is the best outfit or gear anyone could wear. From head to toe, putting on the whole armor of God fully prepares and protects you from battles we face daily, whether it is in your mind, faith, or just your everyday life.

The shield of faith stops the fiery arrows that are designed to destroy you. The shield stops penetration of that which is destructive. When something is bulletproof or even waterproof, it means that nothing can get in to cause damage. It means nothing will be able to seep in or cause what is being protected from becoming affected by outside influence. There is so much negativity that surrounds us daily, and sometimes it is hard to fight against it alone. We need the power of God to be able to stand against the enemies' plans and his devices.

God has given us every tool to empower us to help in this life's journey. Above all, as the Word of God tells us to take up the shield of faith. This faith is not something we hide behind, but it is what we use to divert the wicked schemes of the devil. Just like the soldiers during the ancient times used a shield to fight against their enemies, so are we who believe in God should use our faith to counterattack our enemies. Faith is a powerful tool that no one can take from you.

However, if you do not use these God-given tools, they will lie dormant. To fortify your faith, one must faith proof your life. You have to take inventory of where you are in your faith and as it pertains to your life. Review where you are and see if there is any doubt or fear that has caused you to be stagnant. Have there been any hardships or failures that have caused you to give up and quit? Have negative influences seeped into your life that causes you to act out of character? I encouraged you to face these areas of your life; one by one and faith proof it.

Just like that shield or that bulletproof vest, when you use faith as a protectant, there will be no lie, doubt, adversity, hardship, or obstacles that can penetrate your life. The truth is, things will happen good or bad, but it's how we deal with them when they happen that shows how strong your faith is working for you. Having faith is like having a wall of protection built around you that protects you from every fiery dart that comes your way. All things are possible to them that believe (Mark 9:23 NKJV).

Whatever you are believing God for and whatever visions you desire to see, trust that you can succeed at anything you put your mind to do. It may not be easy, and it may come with challenges, but know that even they are temporary. Keep your eyes on the prize, press pass all the distractions and push past all the doubters until you reach the finish line to your dream.

The key is to have faith in God. It pleases God when we have faith in him, and He rewards us for having it. (Hebrews 11:6) Remember, Faith is now. It is a gift given by God. It brings things to life that were once dead, and it creates what has never been created before and causes it to become something beautiful. Notice the ancient soldiers used their shield to move forward in battle. They did not put up their shield to retreat or walk backward, but they proceeded forward ready and equipped to face whatever battle came their way. Have that kind of faith that moves you forward while at the same time protecting and extinguishing every fiery dart coming your way. Faith Forward!

Faith gives us the victory to overcome trials and tribulations we face. 1 John 5:4 says, "for everyone born of God overcomes the world. This is the victory that has overcome the world, even our faith." Faith overcomes satan and his wicked schemes and plans. Having faith empowers you giving you supernatural strength to push back and demolish strongholds that have been set up to keep you in bondage. It works for you and against your enemies at the same time. Faith is a force to be reckoned with!

Prayer: Dear God, thank you for giving the tools I need to fight against every enemy set up to kill, steal, and destroy my life. Let my faith please you and remind me to always cloth myself daily with the full armor you provide for me so that I can stand and see the salvation of the Lord. Thank you for giving me the victory over all evil in Jesus name Amen.

Encouragement

I pray that this short power-pack book has encouraged, enlightened, and blessed you. I hope your faith has ignited from what you have read in Faith Proof and that you will never walk in fear again. Even as I was writing this book, there were times I wanted to quit because I ran into a few challenges. The enemy tried to derail this assignment, but it did not work because I knew that this would bless someone. Therefore, I say to you, do not quit, and do not give up on your dreams. Go forward in faith and watch what God does through you. God has great things in store for you, and they are right before you. Do not look back and do not rehearse the things of the past. What God has for you is for your future so, walk-in confidence knowing your best days are ahead. God bless you, Shontel Wood

Personal Invitation

If you are reading this book and you have not accepted the Lord Jesus Christ into your life, I would like to invite you to accept Him into your heart today simply repeating this small prayer:

Dear Lord, I come to you with an open heart confessing that I am a sinner who needs your help. Forgive me for all my wrongdoings that I have done to this day and come into my heart and transform me so that I may live the life that you have purposed for me in Jesus name, AMEN.

Romans 10:9-10 "That if you confess with your mouth the Lord Jesus and believe in your heart that God has raised Him from the dead, you will be saved. 10 For with the heart one believes unto righteousness, and with the mouth confession is made unto salvation."

If you have prayed this prayer, you are now a born-again believer. By faith, you are saved. Your life will never be the same again. I pray that you will experience God in ways unimaginable and that His light will shine within you like never before.

Faith Scriptures

"May the God of hope fill you with all joy and peace as you trust in him, so that you may overflow with hope by the power of the Holy Spirit." Romans 15:13 (NIV)

"But when you ask, you must believe and not doubt, because the one who doubts is like a wave of the sea, blown and tossed by the wind." James 1:6 (NIV)

"Though you have not seen him, you love him; and even though you do not see him now, you believe in him and are filled with an inexpressible and glorious joy, for you are receiving the end result of your faith, the salvation of your souls." 1 Peter 1:8-9 (NIV)

"Because you know that the testing of your faith produces perseverance." James 1:3 (NIV)

"If you can'?" said Jesus. "Everything is possible for one who believes." Mark 9:23 (NIV)

"So in Christ Jesus you are all children of God through faith, for all of you who were baptized into Christ have clothed yourselves with Christ." Galatians 3:26-27 (NIV)

"For in the gospel the righteousness of God is revealed—a righteousness that is by faith from first to last, just as it is written: "The righteous will live by faith.""

Romans 1:17 (NIV)

"So then faith comes by hearing, and hearing by the word of God." Romans 10:17 (NKJV)

"That your faith should not be in the wisdom of men but in the power of God." 1 Corinthians 2:5 (NKJV)

"For by grace you have been saved through faith. And this is not your own doing; it is the gift of God, not a result of works, so that no one may boast." Ephesians 2:8-9 (ESV)

"For with God nothing will be impossible." Luke 1:37 (NKJV)

"For as the body without the spirit is dead, so faith without works is dead also." James 2:26 (NKJV)

"You will keep him in perfect peace, Whose mind is stayed on You, Because he trusts in You." Isiah 26:3 (NKJV)

"Fear not, for I am with you; Be not dismayed, for I am your God. I will strengthen you,

Yes, I will help you, I will uphold you with My righteous right hand." Isiah 41:10 (NKJV)

"Be on your guard; stand firm in the faith; be courageous; be strong." 1 Corinthians 16:13 (NIV)

"Looking unto Jesus, the author and finisher of our faith, who for the joy that was set before Him endured the cross, despising the shame, and has sat down at the right hand of the throne of God." Hebrews 12:2 (NKJV)

"By faith the people passed through the Red Sea as on dry land; but when the Egyptians tried to do so, they were drowned." Hebrews 11:29 (NIV)

"By faith the walls of Jericho fell, after the army had marched around them for seven days." Hebrews 11:30 (NIV)

He did not waver at the promise of God through unbelief, but was strengthened in faith, giving glory to God, Romans 4:20 (NIV)

Acknowledgments

I give honor to the Lord Jesus Christ for transforming my life and preserving my life for such a time as this. I am grateful to God that He has given me the ability to write and share with the world how marvelous He is. I would like to give a big thank you to my family and friends for always being supportive of my dreams. God bless you all! This is just the beginning. Stay tuned!

References

Merriam-Webster Dictionary - www.merriam-webster.com

Dictionary.com

BibleGateway.com

Printed in the United States
By Bookmasters